Original title:
Stars Beneath My Pillow

Author: Colin Harrington
ISBN HARDBACK: 978-9916-90-738-2
ISBN PAPERBACK: 978-9916-90-739-9

Hidden Galaxies of Slumber

In veils of night, the stars align,
Soft whispers hush the world divine.
Dreams take flight on moonlit wings,
In slumber's grasp, the heart still sings.

Hidden realms where shadows play,
Golden visions drift away.
Through secret doors of sleep we roam,
In galaxies far, we find our home.

Dreams Adrift in a Velvet Sea

Waves of thoughts in silence glide,
Sailing on a dark tide wide.
Velvet depths, where secrets lie,
Beneath the stars, we drift and fly.

Whispers float on gentle swells,
Carrying tales that memory tells.
In this haven, lost and free,
We weave our dreams in harmony.

Nighttime's Glittering Confessions

Underneath the silver sky,
Stars confess and softly cry.
In their light, the truth unfurls,
Glimmers dance in whispered swirls.

Eager hearts wide open stand,
Revealing secrets, hand in hand.
Through the night, the stories soar,
With each twinkling, we explore.

Ethereal Echoes of the Mind

Fleeting thoughts like shadows pass,
Reflections in a crystal glass.
Ethereal echoes softly play,
Guiding us along the way.

In twilight's glow, the visions blend,
Fragments of dreams around the bend.
Though fleeting, they leave their mark,
Illuminating paths from dark.

Fantasies Woven with Light

In whispers soft, they dance and play,
Bright visions glimmer, night turns to day.
Threads of gold intertwine with dreams,
Painting the sky with shimmering beams.

Stars waltz above in tandem grace,
Holding secrets in their vast space.
Fantasies breathe in the gentle glow,
A tapestry woven, where wonders flow.

Echoes of Cosmic Lullabies

In quiet moments, the universe sings,
Soft lullabies wrapped in cosmic wings.
Melodies drift through the velvet night,
Carried on whispers of distant light.

Galaxies spin in a tender sway,
Echoes weaving a gentle ballet.
Each note a promise, a star's warm kiss,
In dreams we wander, lost in bliss.

Velvet Nights and Galactic Dreams

Under a cloak of dark velvet skies,
The cosmos beckons with sparkly eyes.
Dreams take flight on the wings of dusk,
In the deep silence, there's beauty to trust.

Nebulas swirl like a painter's brush,
While comets streak in a radiant rush.
In velvet nights, we find our way,
Chasing the wonders where stardust lay.

Resting in the Embrace of Infinity

Cradled in shadows, we find our peace,
In infinity's arms, our worries cease.
The universe wraps us in gentle sighs,
Where time dissolves and true beauty lies.

Eons whisper in the silent void,
Creating calm where chaos is avoided.
Resting here, our spirits unite,
In the embrace of the endless night.

The Universe Cradles Me

In silent night, stars gleam bright,
A cradle spun with pure delight.
Galaxies whisper, soft and low,
In their embrace, my worries go.

Winds of cosmic dust flow free,
Carrying dreams, they comfort me.
Time drifts gently, a tender breeze,
Wrapped in magic, I find my peace.

Resting in the Embrace of Infinity

Cradled in shadows, we find our peace,
In infinity's arms, our worries cease.
The universe wraps us in gentle sighs,
Where time dissolves and true beauty lies.

Eons whisper in the silent void,
Creating calm where chaos is avoided.
Resting here, our spirits unite,
In the embrace of the endless night.

The Universe Cradles Me

In silent night, stars gleam bright,
A cradle spun with pure delight.
Galaxies whisper, soft and low,
In their embrace, my worries go.

Winds of cosmic dust flow free,
Carrying dreams, they comfort me.
Time drifts gently, a tender breeze,
Wrapped in magic, I find my peace.

Ethereal Dreams and Cosmic Streams

In visions vast, I wander far,
Through streams of light, I chase a star.
Ethereal whispers, secrets unfold,
Of worlds unknown and tales untold.

The night unfurls its velvet shade,
While dreams awaken, unafraid.
In this realm where shadows dance,
I find my spirit in a trance.

Celestial Serenade in Midnight's Embrace

A serenade of nightingale calls,
With every note, the darkness falls.
In midnight's arms, I find my tune,
Beneath the gaze of a watchful moon.

The stars compose a symphony,
Their harmony envelops me.
In every chord, a heartbeat sways,
As night unfolds its timeless ways.

Glittering Hopes in the Darkness

In shadows deep, where dreams reside,
Glittering hopes refuse to hide.
They shimmer softly, like morning dew,
A promise glows in shades of blue.

As twilight fades, the spirit grows,
With every challenge, courage flows.
Amidst the dark, a light will gleam,
In every heart, a vibrant dream.

Nightfall's Crystal Clusters

Stars twinkle in the vast expanse,
Whispers of the night take their stance.
Moonlight dances on the lake's face,
Bringing dreams to a tranquil space.

Branches sway as shadows play,
Each moment feels like a gentle sway.
In the quiet, secrets unfold,
Night's embrace is a treasure untold.

Luminescent Dreams Unraveled

In the stillness of the midnight air,
Thoughts cascade like a whispered prayer.
Colors blend in a vibrant stream,
Unraveling the fabric of a dream.

Fluttering wings of a waking night,
Illuminate paths with silvery light.
Visions pulse like a beating heart,
Crafting moments that set us apart.

A Tapestry of Silver Wishes

Woven threads in the dark sky,
Carry wishes that softly fly.
Each flicker holds a silent plea,
In the depths of night's decree.

Touched by starlight, we all aspire,
A tapestry born of deep desire.
Silver glimmers in the night's breath,
Creating whispers that conquer death.

Galactic Reveries in the Dark

Nebulae swirl in the cosmic dance,
Dreamers find solace, lose themselves in chance.
Through the void, visions gleam bright,
Guiding the souls in the endless night.

Constellations weave tales of old,
Mysterious stories waiting to be told.
In the darkness, we reach for the light,
Galactic reveries take their flight.

Moonlit Thoughts Among the Clouds

In whispers soft the night does creep,
Upon the clouds where secrets keep.
Laced with silver, dreams take flight,
Guided gently by the moonlight.

Thoughts unravel like shadows cast,
Intertwined with echoes past.
A tapestry of twilight's glow,
Weaving tales the stars bestow.

Soft Stardust on Evening Tides

Waves embrace the shore with grace,
Carrying whispers of a distant place.
Stardust dances on the breeze,
Filling hearts with gentle ease.

The ocean sighs a lullaby,
As constellations fill the sky.
A fusion of dreams and light,
Glimmers softly through the night.

Galactic Echoes in My Sleep

Upon the pillow, thoughts take wing,
In the vastness, dreams will sing.
Galaxies pulse with radiant hue,
Whispering secrets old and new.

As night descends, the silence speaks,
In cosmic realms, my spirit seeks.
In slumber's grasp, I drift away,
To where the stars forever play.

Chasing Shadows of the Night

Through alleyways where echoes lie,
I chase the shadows drifting by.
Each step a tale, each breath a sigh,
In the moon's embrace, we quietly fly.

Mysterious paths that twist and turn,
In the heart of night, the lanterns burn.
With whispered hopes, we weave our flight,
Chasing dreams beneath the light.

Cosmic Glow of Nighttime Dreams

In the quiet hours, stars ignite,
Whispers of dreams in silver light.
Galaxies dance, a waltz so bright,
Nights unfurl with endless delight.

Moonlit shadows begin to play,
Guiding thoughts that drift away.
In cosmic realms where wishes stay,
Hearts embrace the Milky Way.

Ethereal Light Under My Head

Resting softly on whispers of night,
An embrace as soft as starlit flight.
Ethereal light fills the room with grace,
Dreams begin their gentle race.

Stars like fragments of wishes glow,
In tresses of time, they ebb and flow.
Under my head, a cosmic show,
A world of wonder begins to grow.

Dreams Dressed in Celestial Gown

Softly dressed in twilight's hue,
Dreams unfurl in night's debut.
Celestial gowns that shimmer bright,
Holding secrets of the night.

They twirl in rhythms of silent tunes,
Beneath the watchful, glowing moons.
In this realm, where fantasy looms,
Magic lingers, and heart resumes.

Milky Way's Soft Embrace

In the stillness, the cosmos breathes,
Milky Way's embrace, the heart believes.
Stars drop softly, like whispered lines,
Crafting stories in celestial designs.

Cradled in night's gentle sway,
Dreams take flight on silver rays.
Through the void, our spirits play,
In Milky Way's soft embrace, we stay.

Celestial Secrets in Slumber

In the hush of night's embrace,
Stars weave tales in whispered grace.
Dreams take flight on silver beams,
Painting shadows of our dreams.

Crimson skies and velvet hues,
Bathe the world in mystic views.
Each heartbeat echoes in the dark,
Guiding souls to realms that spark.

Dreams of Distant Constellations

Beyond the veil of sleep we roam,
In galaxies so far from home.
Whispers from the cosmic sea,
Lead us to our destiny.

Nebulae in colors bright,
Shimmer softly in the night.
With every wish upon a star,
We feel their pull from afar.

Nightfall's Guiding Light

As day surrenders to night's grace,
A gentle quiet fills the space.
Luna's glow, a beacon bright,
Illuminates the path of light.

With every star that starts to gleam,
We find our way in woven dreams.
In silence, secrets come alive,
Within our hearts, the wishes thrive.

A Tapestry of Celestial Dreams

Weaving threads of stardust bright,
Crafting visions in the night.
Each glimmer tells a story old,
Of wonders waiting to unfold.

In the cosmos, we find our peace,
Where worries cease and troubles decrease.
With every breath, we touch the sky,
Dancing dreams on wings that fly.

Cosmic Hugs at Dusk's Doorstep

The sun dips low, a golden thread,
Whispers of night, softly spread.
Stars begin their gentle glow,
Embracing dreams as breezes flow.

In this hush, the world slows down,
Wrapped in twilight's shimmering gown.
Each heartbeat resonates in time,
With the universe, a silent rhyme.

Moonlight spills on the quiet ground,
In this magic, love is found.
Cosmic hugs, where hearts entwine,
In the vastness, spirits shine.

As dusk becomes a tender night,
Warmth unfurls, a soft, sweet light.
Together we will drift and sway,
In cosmic arms, forever stay.

The Night's Embrace and the Endless Sky

Under stars that brightly gleam,
The night enfolds a hopeful dream.
With every breath, the cosmos sings,
A tale of love and wondrous things.

The moon, a guardian in the dark,
Ignites the night with its silver spark.
Whispers of secrets, soft and sweet,
Guide weary souls with rhythmic beat.

Through fields of clouds, we gently drift,
A dance of shadows, a tender gift.
The horizon melts in shades of blue,
Wrapped in the sky, just me and you.

Hold my hand as we share the view,
Infinity beckons, vast and true.
In the night's embrace, we find our place,
Lost in the magic, a warm embrace.

Navigating Waves of Stardust in Sleep

As night descends, the world transforms,
Softly wrapped in galaxy's arms.
Dreamers sail on waves of light,
Navigating through the velvet night.

Starry whispers call us near,
In this realm, there's nothing to fear.
Time suspends, the moments blend,
In stardust tides, our spirits mend.

Eyes shut tight, yet visions soar,
Into the cosmos, forevermore.
Drifting through nebulae so bright,
We find our dreams beneath the night.

In slumber's depth, we freely roam,
Across the stars, we find our home.
In waves of wonder, we take flight,
Navigating stardust, pure delight.

Dreams Whisper in the Night

In shadows deep, the whispers call,
Of dreams that dance and softly fall.
They float on air, like feathered sighs,
A tapestry spun where silence lies.

Beneath the moon's watchful gaze,
They twirl and weave in a mystic haze.
With every breath, they paint the dark,
A symphony bright, a fleeting spark.

Through tangled thoughts, the visions glide,
On wings of hope, they gently ride.
Awakening hearts to tales untold,
In the night's embrace, their magic bold.

So let them soar, let dreams take flight,
In whispered tones, they guide the night.
A pathway paved with stardust gleam,
Where every moment feels like a dream.

Celestial Secrets Unfurled

In the silence of the cosmic sea,
Stars unveil their mysteries free.
Whispers of ancient tales resound,
Where lost constellations still abound.

Between the worlds of dusk and dawn,
Hidden truths linger, softly drawn.
Galaxies spin in a timeless dance,
Inviting all to take a chance.

The planets hum their vibrant song,
In harmony where dreams belong.
Veils of night, the secrets keep,
As celestial wonders softly leap.

Unfurled like sails on cosmic seas,
These secrets sway with gentle breeze.
Embrace the vast, embrace the light,
And journey forth through endless night.

Midnight's Luminous Embrace

Under the veil of midnight's grace,
The world is kissed by a tender trace.
A glow that wraps the earth in peace,
In quiet whispers, worries cease.

Stars ignite in the deep blue skies,
Sparkling dreams in wandering eyes.
The moonlight drapes in silken threads,
Awakening stories long left unsaid.

Through shadows cast, the soft light gleams,
Kindling fires of forgotten dreams.
Each heartbeat echoes a soft refrain,
In luminous embrace, love will remain.

So linger here in this sacred night,
Where every moment feels just right.
In the arms of darkness, we find our space,
And dance beneath midnight's warm embrace.

Cosmic Thoughts on Ivory

On sheets of ivory, thoughts take flight,
Carried away in the depths of night.
Stars are scattered like ink on a page,
Where cosmic musings softly engage.

Each line a glimpse of a distant star,
Memories beckon from afar.
Galaxies spin in a quiet tune,
Painting dreams beneath the moon.

In every curve, a story told,
Of love and loss, of truth and bold.
With each stroke, the universe sways,
In harmony where time decays.

So write your thoughts, let the magic flow,
On ivory's canvas, let feelings grow.
For in each word, a light shall gleam,
Weaving paths within a cosmic dream.

Dreaming of Faraway Galaxies

Stars whisper secrets so bright,
In the silence of the night.
Across the vast and endless skies,
I find comfort in their lies.

Waves of stardust swirl around,
In the darkness, I am found.
Cosmic winds, they softly blow,
Guiding me where dreams can go.

Planets spin with tales untold,
Adventures waiting to unfold.
In my heart, a spark ignites,
Taking flight on endless nights.

I close my eyes, I drift away,
To worlds where shadows dance and sway.
The universe wraps me in grace,
In faraway galaxies, I find my place.

A Bed of Wishes and Wishes Afloat

On a bed of dreams I lay,
Wishes weave like night and day.
Floating high, they twirl and spin,
A dance of hope, where dreams begin.

Each thought a feather, soft and light,
Carried on the breeze of night.
Casting wishes, one by one,
Underneath the silvered sun.

In the silence, magic blooms,
Filling quiet, empty rooms.
With every wish, a heartbeat grows,
As joy inside my spirit flows.

A tapestry of hopes entwined,
In this moment, peace I find.
Wishes drift on gentle streams,
A bed of wishes, cradle dreams.

Remnants of Light in My Rest

Softly fading, the light descends,
Caressing shadows, it gently bends.
In the stillness, the echoes play,
Remnants of light at the end of day.

Dreams linger like whispers in air,
Carried on hope, a silent prayer.
Illuminated thoughts take flight,
Awakening the depths of night.

Stars embedded in memory's maze,
A glimmering path, a hopeful gaze.
Resting now, I find release,
In the remnants, I seek my peace.

As the moon's glow softly sighs,
I surrender to the night skies.
In slumber's arms, I drift and weave,
Finding solace in what I believe.

Cosmic Dust on My Dreams

Cosmic dust settles like snow,
Whispering secrets only I know.
In the twilight, dreams reveal,
A universe that feels so real.

Trailing starlight, I take flight,
Soaring high into the night.
Each twinkle holds a memory told,
Adventures painted in shades of gold.

With each heartbeat, galaxies spin,
Infinite journeys waiting within.
I gather stardust, pure and bright,
To weave my thoughts into the night.

In the quiet, I find my voice,
Among the stars, I make my choice.
Cosmic dust on my dreams will stay,
Guiding my soul through night and day.

Light Trails in the Quiet Night

Stars flicker in the velvet sky,
Whispers of the nighttime breeze flow.
Moonbeams dance on shadows shy,
Guiding hearts where dreams may go.

Footsteps soft on midnight's path,
Echoes of a world unseen.
Each moment's glow, a gentle laugh,
Lost in starlight's silver sheen.

Enchanted Dreams

In twilight's arms, the visions glide,
Softly weaving tales so bright.
With every heartbeat, hopes collide,
Creating magic in the night.

Whimsical paths of vibrant hues,
Carried by the moonlit stream.
In these dreams, we find our muse,
Awakening to wonder's scheme.

Wandering Wishes

Beneath the stars, our wishes soar,
Like kites on an endless flight.
Carried far to distant shores,
Their glimmers spark the quiet night.

Each dream a star, a beacon bright,
In the canvas of the dark.
They call to us with gentle light,
Igniting hope, a guiding spark.

The Memory of Light in My Slumber

In the depths of sleep, I find,
Fragments of a golden glow.
Whispers of a day unkind,
Yet hope's warm embers gently grow.

Dreams hold remnants of the past,
Softly cradling what has been.
In the shadows, echoes cast,
A reminder of the light within.

Celestial Maps on a Sea of Thoughts

Upon the ocean of my mind,
The stars align, a roadmap clear.
Navigating dreams combined,
Where every thought draws you near.

Celestial bodies swirl and sway,
Guiding ships through realms unknown.
In the silence of the fray,
We sail until the dawn is shown.

Nighttime's Hidden Wonders

Stars whisper secrets in the night,
Dreams awaken, taking flight.
The moonlight dances on the ground,
In shadows deep, magic is found.

Crickets sing their lullaby,
While fireflies twinkle in the sky.
The world quiets, all is still,
As mystery unfolds at will.

Every rustle tells a tale,
Of nighttime journeys, soft and pale.
The cool breeze carries a scent,
Of nature's breath, wild and bent.

Embrace the dark, let go of fear,
In the night, wonders appear.
Open your heart to the unseen,
Find the beauty where it's been.

Astral Sighs in the Silence

In the hush of the midnight glow,
Celestial dreams begin to flow.
Comets race across the skies,
Stardust drifts with silent sighs.

Each twinkle holds a tale untold,
Of ancient worlds and treasures old.
Floating softly, thoughts entwine,
Lost in the dance of the divine.

Nebulae paint in shades so bright,
Whispers echo through the night.
Galaxies spin in endless grace,
A timeless rhythm we embrace.

Capture moments, let them glide,
In cosmic dreams, let hope reside.
With every breath, connect the dots,
In the silence, find what's sought.

Moonlit Whispers of Imagination

Beneath the moon, ideas bloom,
Imagination fills the room.
Each flicker of light, a spark so clear,
Inviting us to wander near.

Stories linger in the night air,
Whispered dreams we all can share.
Characters dance, they come alive,
With magic's touch, our minds will thrive.

Soft shadows play upon the ground,
In their embrace, our hopes are found.
A tapestry woven with delight,
We paint our visions in silver light.

In the stillness, let thoughts roam,
Crafting tales of a world unknown.
With every heartbeat, let them flow,
In moonlit whispers, let them grow.

The Universe Tucked Away

In corners dark, the cosmos sleeps,
Secrets held in silence deep.
Galaxies hide, waiting for eyes,
To unveil wonders in disguise.

Every star a flicker of fate,
Celestial patterns we contemplate.
Time holds its breath, a tender pause,
Unraveling truths, without cause.

Auroras dance in vibrant hues,
A hidden symphony of the muse.
The universe knows of dreams we share,
Crafted in stardust, light as air.

Listen close for the softest call,
In the hush of night, we find it all.
With open hearts, we look within,
In the realm of dreams, we begin.

Echoes of a Universe Afar

Stars whisper tales in the night,
Winds carry wishes in flight.
Galaxies spin in a dance,
Sending dreams on a chance.

Nebulas glow with vibrant grace,
Time bends gently in this space.
Hearts drift wide across the sky,
Boundless freedom, we can fly.

Light-years travel through the dark,
Each sparkle's a distant mark.
In silence, we learn to hear,
Echoes of those we hold dear.

A universe vast and profound,
In its arms, we are unbound.
Each moment a cosmic thread,
Woven softly, love widespread.

The Night Sky's Gentle Kiss

The moon wraps the earth in light,
Whispers secrets, calm and bright.
Stars twinkle down from above,
A canvas painted with love.

Crickets sing their softest tune,
Beneath the watchful gaze of the moon.
Night's embrace is warm and wide,
In this serenity, we abide.

Clouds drift lazily, dreams take flight,
Hearts unite in the still night.
The sky's gentle kiss, a grace,
Makes the world a sacred place.

Sleep comes easy, minds unwind,
In the solace, comfort we find.
The night wraps its arms around,
In this love, forever bound.

Lullabies of the Milky Way

Galaxies hum a gentle tune,
Notes flow softly, like a boon.
Stardust falls in a tender sigh,
Lullabies weave through the sky.

Cradled in cosmic arms so wide,
Dreamers wander, hearts open wide.
Planets spin in a silent sway,
Guiding wishes along the way.

Celestial whispers touch the mind,
In the stillness, peace we find.
The Milky Way sings all night,
With its shimmering strands of light.

Close your eyes to the cosmic song,
In this space, we all belong.
Lullabies of stars so bright,
Carry us through the endless night.

Astral Nightmares and Quiet Dreams

In shadows deep, where fears abide,
Nightmares creep, they cannot hide.
Yet through the gloom, dreams softly scheme,
We find light in the darkest theme.

Stars flicker, both bright and dim,
Each one telling tales grim.
In the tapestry of night,
Hope emerges, taking flight.

Echoes of fears fade away,
As we're wrapped in night's ballet.
Quiet dreams hold us tight,
Guided by the moon's soft light.

Astral realms beckon, both fierce and sweet,
In this balance, our hearts beat.
With each breath, nightmares dissolve,
In quiet dreams, we evolve.

Starlit Fantasies on Silk Sheets

Whispers of night in silver glow,
Dreams unfurl where shadows flow.
Crickets sing a lullaby sweet,
Lost in thoughts where heartbeats meet.

Fingers trace the patterns of stars,
As we dance beneath Venus and Mars.
Embroidered wishes in twilight's seam,
Together we weave the fabric of dream.

The moon spills secrets on the floor,
Each sigh a tale, a love encore.
Wrapped in warmth of silk's embrace,
Time stands still in this sacred space.

With starlit fantasies, we're intertwined,
In a realm where love is blind.
We drift on clouds, let worry cease,
In this moment, we find our peace.

Constellation's Caress

Under a blanket of cosmic light,
The universe holds us tight.
We trace the lines of ancient skies,
Finding solace in soft sighs.

Every twinkle, a lover's vow,
Promises painted upon the bough.
In this dance of gravity's pull,
Our hearts become forever full.

Galaxies whisper, secrets to share,
As we drift through the cool night air.
The stars above softly embrace,
Each glimmer penned in celestial grace.

In this cosmic love so free,
We are where we're meant to be.
The constellation's caress we feel,
In each heartbeat, the infinite real.

Dreamscapes of the Infinite

Floating through corridors of time,
In dreamscapes where silence chimes.
Colors meld in spectral hues,
With whispers lost in the evening blues.

Every shadow a story untold,
Magic weaves through dreamlike gold.
A tapestry of wishes we spin,
Where every journey begins within.

Infinity dances in our sight,
Stars align, igniting the night.
Together we roam in worlds unseen,
Chasing the echoes of what has been.

In dreams we find lost pieces of fate,
The universe curious and sedate.
With each step, a memory speaks,
In dreamscapes, our spirit peaks.

A Pillow of Comets and Dreams

Upon this pillow, dreams ignite,
Comets blaze through the quiet night.
Resting under a cosmic dome,
In this shelter, we are home.

Visions dance like starlit fire,
Each spark a whisper of desire.
As galaxies spin, we drift away,
Lost in the magic of dreams we play.

The heartbeat of the universe sings,
Cradling us in celestial wings.
Every breath a wish, a scheme,
Sailing together on the river of dream.

A pillow of comets cradles our heads,
Through cosmic pathways, our spirit spreads.
In a glow of twilight, we find our place,
As dreams and stars intertwine in grace.

The Universe Cradled in Rest

Stars softly gleam in the dark,
Gentle whispers from worlds afar.
Galaxies wrapped in a silent embrace,
Time holds its breath in this vast space.

Nebulas swirl, a colorful dance,
Cradling dreams in a cosmic expanse.
Planets drift in their quiet flight,
Wrapped calmly in the arms of night.

Celestial bodies weave a tale,
Of distant journeys and starlit trails.
In the stillness, a profound peace,
A lullaby that will never cease.

Cosmic Dust on My Mind

Thoughts like stardust swirl around,
In the vastness, they can be found.
Each shimmering speck a whispered wish,
Carried on the cosmic tide's swish.

Galactic echoes fill the air,
With secrets that the night lays bare.
In every shimmer, a story lies,
Winking gently from velvet skies.

As I ponder this stellar mist,
Each particle a fleeting twist.
In the silence, my dreams ignite,
Dust of cosmos in the night.

Whispers of a Dreaming Sky

Clouds like cotton, drifting slow,
Carrying secrets we long to know.
Beneath their shadows, dreams are spun,
Whispers travel, the night begun.

Stars are the wishes of those unseen,
In the stillness, they brightly glean.
Each glimmering dot a tiny spark,
Illuminating the endless dark.

With every breeze, a story flows,
From the heavens where the night wind blows.
The sky, a canvas for our dreams,
In its embrace, nothing is as it seems.

Cosmic Comfort in the Night

Under the veil of twilight's grace,
The universe wraps us in its embrace.
Countless stars twinkle with delight,
As they guide us through the night.

Moonbeams dance on the ocean's face,
A soothing rhythm, a gentle lace.
In this silence, peace takes flight,
Carried softly on cool winds' light.

Every twinkle holds a promise dear,
Of cosmic love that draws us near.
In the night's arms, we find our place,
Comforted by the universe's grace.

Galactic Comforts of the Night

Stars twinkle softly in the vast sky,
Moon whispers secrets, as the night sighs.
A blanket of silence envelops the ground,
In this stillness, pure solace is found.

Dreams take flight on cosmic waves,
Wandering souls on starlit graves.
Galactic wonders, secrets unfold,
Night's embrace, a blessing untold.

Enchanted Darkness of My Thoughts

In shadows deep where wonders sleep,
Thoughts entwine in silence, secrets to keep.
Each notion dances, a flickering flame,
In the enchanted dark, they call my name.

Whispers of dusk weave tales anew,
Journeys begin in soft shades of blue.
The heart finds peace in the quiet depth,
In the enchanting night, I take a breath.

Dreamscapes Drifting Above

Clouds of cotton, dreams interlace,
Drifting gently through time and space.
Visions collide in a whimsical play,
As the mind wanders, night turns to day.

Floating softly, the past and the now,
In this surreal place, I take a bow.
Dreamscapes glimmer like stars in the night,
Guiding the heart with their luminous light.

Celestial Hues on Fabric Threads

Woven in colors of twilight's grace,
Each thread tells stories from a faraway place.
Celestial hues paint the fabric bright,
In this tapestry, dreams take flight.

Stitches of wonder in each soft fold,
Whispers of magic, timeless and bold.
On this canvas of night, my heart expands,
Embracing the cosmos with open hands.

Galactic Wings Wrapped Around

In the quiet of the night,
Stars twinkle bright,
Galaxies swirl in flight,
Cosmic dreams take flight.

Wrapped in shades of blue,
Celestial hues so true,
Gentle whispers of the few,
Infinity calls anew.

With every breath we take,
The universe starts to wake,
We dance on the edge of fate,
In this magic we partake.

Across the vast unknown,
Together we have grown,
Carried by a cosmic drone,
Our spirits freely flown.

Night's Embrace of Heavenly Wishes

Under the blanket of stars,
Dreams ignite, love's memoirs,
Whispers flow from afar,
Night's magic opens doors.

Every wish cast on high,
Soars like birds in the sky,
In silence, we sigh,
As moments gently fly.

The moon's soft silver light,
Guides us through the night,
With hope shining bright,
Our hearts take flight.

In the stillness, we find,
A peace intertwined,
Heavenly love defined,
In dreams, we are enshrined.

Hidden Wonders in the Stillness

In the hush of dawn's gleam,
Whispers awaken a dream,
Nature's soft, gentle scheme,
Cradled in a golden beam.

Hidden wonders come alive,
In stillness, spirits thrive,
Where mysteries quietly dive,
Creating blissful jive.

The rustle of leaves nearby,
Beneath the vast, azure sky,
Inviting us to fly,
To places unseen, awry.

Each moment, a treasure found,
In silence, we are bound,
With every heartbeat sound,
Revelations profound.

Cosmic Whispers in the Dark

In shadows, secrets dwell,
Cosmic stories to tell,
Under the moon's gentle spell,
In the silence, we quell.

Stars twinkle, soft and deep,
As night begins to creep,
Into our hearts they seep,
In dreams, together we leap.

Galactic echoes all around,
In the dark, connections found,
With every breath, a sound,
In this unity, we're crowned.

Let us dance within the night,
Guided by celestial light,
In whispers, take our flight,
Through the cosmos, pure delight.

Celestial Cradles and Soft Sleeps

In quiet nights where stars softly gleam,
Cradles of light weave the fabric of dreams.
Gentle whispers touch the velvety air,
Wrapped in the warmth of love without care.

Moonlight dances on the sleepy trees,
Swaying softly with the night's gentle breeze.
In the arms of the cosmos, we safely drift,
Finding solace in the universe's gift.

Each twinkling light sings a lullaby sweet,
As shadows gather, the day takes a seat.
Celestial cradles hold hearts without fear,
In this vast expanse, we find peace here.

Whispers Between the Moonbeams

Beneath a sky where whispers flutter by,
Moonbeams glisten, painting dreams in the sky.
They carry tales of love across the night,
Inviting hearts to share in their light.

Each shimmer holds secrets, soft and profound,
In the stillness, their magic is found.
Glimmers of hope trail through the dark haze,
Guiding lost souls in an ethereal blaze.

Between the shadows, stories intertwine,
In tranquil moments, our spirits align.
With every breath, we dance through the glow,
Wrapped in the whispers only night can bestow.

A Journey through the Infinite Sky

On wings of dreams, we soar through the night,
Across the canvas of starlit delight.
Each twinkle beckons, a call to explore,
A journey awaits, opening each door.

Galaxies spiral in a cosmic embrace,
Timeless voyages in this vast, sacred space.
With every heartbeat, the universe sings,
As we navigate through the wonders it brings.

The colors of dusk blend with dawn's gentle hues,
In this boundless realm, we let go of blues.
Riding the currents of the infinite sea,
Finding our place in this grand tapestry.

Veiled in Midnight's Mystery

The night drapes softly, a cloak made of dreams,
Veiled in moonlight, it silently gleams.
Whispers of shadows weave tales to be told,
In midnight's grasp, the world feels bold.

Stars overhead, like lanterns they shine,
Each one a story, a thread divine.
Mysteries linger in the cool night air,
Inviting us deeper, to wander and stare.

With hearts open wide, we embrace the unknown,
In midnight's embrace, we find we are home.
Lost in the wonder, we drift without fear,
Veiled in the magic that dances so near.

Mysteries of the Midnight Veil

Whispers glide through shadowed trees,
Stars flicker with secrets carried by the breeze.
Moonlight dances on a silver stream,
Inviting all to dream a dream.

Fog wraps around the ancient ground,
In silence, lost truths are found.
Ghostly echoes fill the night,
Enigmas hidden from the light.

A figure moves with graceful ease,
Wrapped in fabric that sways with the leaves.
The midnight veil conceals the past,
Yet reveals the wonder through shadows cast.

Eyes that shimmer in the dark,
Each gaze ignites a forgotten spark.
In the velvet of night, mysteries bloom,
Awakening thoughts that dispel the gloom.

The Dreams that Traverse the Cosmos

Galaxies twirl in a dance so grand,
Across time and space, we hold their hand.
Nebulas shimmer, colors collide,
Each dream a journey, a cosmic ride.

Planets whisper with voices sweet,
Echoes of stardust beneath our feet.
A universe wide, a canvas so vast,
Tracing the dreams of our shadowed past.

Constellations weave tales in the sky,
Guiding our hearts as we aim to fly.
In the silence, a symphony plays,
Riding the waves of celestial bays.

Connect the stars with threads of gold,
Stories of love and adventure unfold.
In dreams that traverse the endless night,
We find our selves in the cosmic light.

Veils of Night and Heavenly Light

Darkness wraps the world in a shroud,
Softly lifting as twilight bows down.
Heavenly light seeps through the veil,
A tapestry woven with wonders to unveil.

Stars peek through the fabric of night,
Each glimmer a wish, each twinkle a light.
Veils of night hold stories untold,
Of journeys begun in dreams bright and bold.

The moon drapes the earth in silvery lace,
With gentle whispers, it warms the space.
Celestial bodies waltz on high,
Beneath their glow, fears drift and die.

In the embrace of night, we find grace,
Radiance hidden in each shadow's place.
Veils of night lift to reveal our fate,
In the light of the stars, we captivate.

Slumbering within Celestial Realms

Dreamers lie still, in twilight's embrace,
Slumbering softly in a starry lace.
Celestial realms where the heart takes flight,
Guided by visions that dance in the night.

Among the comets, our spirits soar,
Exploring the wonders of the cosmic lore.
Stars hum a lullaby, tender and bright,
Cradling our dreams till dawn's gentle light.

In the silence of space, time stands still,
Whispers of galaxies, soft and shrill.
Each heartbeat echoes in this endless sea,
Where slumbering souls dream to be free.

When morning arrives, the dreams fade away,
Yet their essence remains, a shimmering spray.
For within the celestial, we find our way,
Awakening our spirits to greet the new day.

A Night's Journey Among the Clouds

In the velvet darkness, whispers fly,
Stars like lanterns in the sky.
A gentle breeze begins to sway,
Guiding hearts along their way.

Clouds drift softly, dreams take flight,
Moonbeams weaving through the night.
Each sigh a story, softly spun,
A tapestry of joy begun.

Echoes of laughter, lost in space,
Time pauses in this sacred place.
Moments captured, still and bright,
In this realm, we find our light.

A night's journey, vast and wide,
With the stars as our guide.
Together we shall always find,
Eternal peace, our souls aligned.

Breezes of the Universe Through My Dreams

In the quiet hush of twilight's grace,
Galaxies bloom, an endless space.
Breezes whisper ancient tales,
Carried through the cosmic gales.

Dreams unfurl like petals' dance,
Drawing thoughts in a trance.
Cosmic winds that softly sigh,
Hold the secrets of the sky.

Starlight twinkles in my eyes,
A universe that never lies.
Each breath a heartbeat, deep and true,
Guiding me to realms anew.

In my slumber, horizons wide,
I embrace the cosmic tide.
With every dream, I softly soar,
To explore the universe's core.

The Universe in My Quiet Moments

In silence deep, I find my peace,
The universe begins to cease.
Stars align in stillness bright,
A cosmic dance, a whisper light.

Thoughts drift freely, like stardust grains,
In this hush, a journey reigns.
Galactic echoes call my name,
In quiet moments, love's the same.

Connections formed in silent space,
Every heartbeat finds its place.
Life unfolds like cosmos wide,
In stillness, there's naught to hide.

The universe, my faithful friend,
In quiet, it begins to mend.
As I breathe, I feel the sway,
Of eternity in every day.

Mental Paths to a Celestial Dance

Through thoughts I wander, paths of light,
Mental journeys take to flight.
Celestial realms where echoes twine,
Waltzing with the grand design.

In shadows cast by thoughts of old,
New visions bloom, a sight to behold.
With every step, the stars align,
In this dance, the universe shines.

Thoughts transcend the earthly ground,
In every heartbeat, peace is found.
A celestial ballet, swift and free,
In mental paths, I long to be.

Together we twirl, in cosmic tune,
Under the glow of the silver moon.
Each thought a note in life's grand song,
In this dance, we all belong.

Moonbeam Reflections on Soft Pillows

In the quiet night's embrace,
Moonlight dances, soft and bright.
Whispers linger on the lace,
Dreams take flight in silver light.

Restful sighs on fabrics weave,
With each glow, a tale unfolds.
In this space, we gently leave,
The world behind, as night enfolds.

Shadows play along the wall,
Crickets serenade the night.
In this grace, we hear the call,
Of peace wrapped in moonbeam's light.

Wrapped in dreams, we softly drift,
Pillows cradle thoughts anew.
In this moment, hearts uplift,
By the glow of moonlit dew.

The Light That Guides My Sleep

In the dark where stillness reigns,
A flicker glows, a gentle spark.
Guiding me through thought's terrains,
Illuminating paths so stark.

Each beam whispers solace sweet,
Carrying dreams upon its flight.
In my heart, I find my seat,
With the light that guides my night.

Softly flowing, as I rest,
In this warm, embracing glow.
It cradles me, a soothing vest,
As the world outside moves slow.

With every breath, I sink so deep,
In this warmth where worries cease.
This is where my spirit leaps,
In the light that grants me peace.

Flickers of Light in the Shadows

Flickers soft, in corners hide,
Shadows cast a mystic game.
Within the dark, where dreams abide,
The spark of hope ignites its flame.

With each flicker, tales unfold,
Moments caught in twilight's grasp.
In the quiet, whispers bold,
Reveal the dreams we long to clasp.

A lantern glows amidst the night,
Guiding hearts through paths unknown.
In its warmth, we find delight,
As flickers dance and brightly shone.

These fragments spark our inner quest,
Leading us to realms of peace.
In shadows deep, we feel the best,
Finding joy as fears release.

Ethereal Glow in the Silent Hours

In the stillness, whispers play,
An ethereal glow ignites the dark.
Casting dreams that drift away,
Illuminating every spark.

Moments framed in silver light,
Painted softly on the wall.
In this realm where dreams take flight,
The silent hours gently call.

Through the night, we softly weave,
Threads of thought in glowing hue.
In the dusk, we learn to believe,
In the magic that shines true.

As dawn approaches, we embrace,
The echoes of the night's sweet song.
In this glow, we find our place,
Where our dreams can linger long.

Pocket of Light in the Heart of Night

In shadows deep, a spark does glow,
A gentle warmth, a calming flow.
It whispers hope through endless dark,
A tiny flame, a guiding mark.

When silence wraps the world in still,
This beacon shines, it bends my will.
With every heartbeat, courage grows,
A pocket of light, forever glows.

Through darkest hours, I find my way,
In the quiet, I will stay.
Each twinkle is a promise bright,
A pocket of light in the heart of night.

Reflections of Infinity in a Dream

In the stillness, dreams take flight,
Through whispered thoughts, in soft twilight.
Endless echoes in the vast unknown,
Reflections of infinity gently sewn.

A tapestry of stars unfolds,
With secrets whispered, stories told.
In every shimmer, a world anew,
Connected threads in midnight's hue.

I drift on waves of silence deep,
Where time dissolves, and shadows seep.
In this realm, reality bends,
Reflections of infinity never ends.

A Universe Wrapped Around Me

Galaxies swirl in a cosmic embrace,
Stars twinkle softly, a timeless grace.
In the vastness, I feel so small,
Yet infinitely held within it all.

Nebulas dance in colors bright,
Painting the canvas of endless night.
In every heartbeat, a cosmic thread,
A universe wrapped around me, spread.

With each breath, I find my place,
Amongst the asteroids, the stars' trace.
In the silence, I touch the divine,
A universe, forever intertwined.

Unraveled Dreams and Cosmic Streams

Beneath the moon, where shadows play,
Unraveled dreams drift far away.
Like whispers lost on a starlit breeze,
They weave through night with effortless ease.

Cosmic streams of thoughts collide,
In gentle waves, my dreams reside.
With every pulse, the cosmos wakes,
As hope ignites with every quake.

In the night sky's vast tapestry,
Each thread connects, from you to me.
Unraveled dreams in the twilight loom,
A dance of worlds in the heart's bloom.

Slumber's Radiant Treasures

In dreams, the whispers softly weave,
A tapestry of stars that never leave.
Beneath the veil of night's tender glow,
Lies a world where hidden wonders flow.

Gentle waves of solace gently swell,
In the heart's embrace, secrets dwell.
Each sigh a promise, a silken thread,
Binding the light where moonbeams tread.

Though dawn may chase the shadows away,
These treasures linger in soft play.
Slumber's gifts, both precious and rare,
A radiant glow within the air.

Awake, the soul reclaims its flight,
Held by the glow of the starlit night.
In the gentle hush, dreams softly say,
Discover the treasures that guide your way.

,

The Starlight Beneath My Head

Resting lightly on a bed of light,
Starlight dances, a comforting sight.
Whispers of cosmos cradle my dream,
In this celestial glow, I am free to gleam.

A gentle hush wraps the world around,
In the quiet, peace and hope are found.
Each twinkle above a story untold,
Beneath my head, the universe unfolds.

Murmurs twist through the cool night air,
As soft as silk, light beyond compare.
My heart beats steadily, a soothing song,
In this realm of starlight, I belong.

With every breath, the night breathes back,
Guiding my dreams on their shimmering track.
I surrender to the deep sky's bed,
Beneath these stars, my spirit is led.

Celestial Reflections in Moonlight

In the moon's embrace, shadows play,
Silver beams weave through night and day.
Reflections dance on the tranquil lake,
A mirror of dreams, where souls awake.

Ripples whisper tales of the deep,
Carried by breezes, secrets they keep.
Moonlight bathes the world in soft gleam,
Inviting all wanderers to dream.

Each ray of light paints an ethereal scene,
Enchanting the dark with its soft sheen.
Celestial bodies in silent chorus,
Guiding the lost, their light bore us.

In this sacred glow, hearts intertwine,
The night unveils stories divine.
Celestial reflections linger and flow,
In moonlit spaces, our spirits grow.

Wandering Through Cosmic Fantasies

In the vast expanse where galaxies spin,
I wander freely, where dreams begin.
Each starlit path, a tale to explore,
In cosmic realms, I yearn for more.

With comets trailing vibrant streams,
I drift through the fabric of woven dreams.
Nebulae swirl in colors so bright,
They paint the canvas of endless night.

As I traverse this celestial sea,
A symphony plays, just for me.
Hope glimmers amidst distant light,
Guiding my heart through the endless night.

In this journey, I find my place,
Among the stars, a warm embrace.
Wandering through cosmic wonders, I soar,
In the dance of infinity, I long for more.

9 789916 907382